FLAGS
OF THE WORLD

HOW TO USE THIS BOOK

Look at the maps in the twelve-page booklet. Using the labels beside each country's sticker, choose the flag that best fits in the space available on the map.

•

Don't forget that your stickers can be stuck down and peeled off again. If you are careful, you can use your flag stickers more than once.

•

You can also use the stickers to decorate school projects or your own books.

LONDON, NEW YORK, MELBOURNE, MUNICH, AND DELHI

First American Edition, 1993
This revised edition, 2012

Published in the United States by DK Publishing, 345 Hudson Street, New York, New York 10014

14 15   10 9 8 7 6 5 4

006—183593—Feb/2012

Published in Great Britain by Dorling Kindersley Limited.

A catalog record for this book is available from the Library of Congress.

ISBN 978-0-7566-9088-5

DK books are available at special discounts when purchased in bulk for sales promotions, premiums, fund-raising, or educational use. For details, contact: DK Publishing Special Markets, 345 Hudson Street, New York, New York 10014 or SpecialSales@dk.com.

Printed and bound in China by L. Rex

Discover more at
www.dk.com

Europe

ICELAND

ATLANTIC
OCEAN

Faeroe Islands
(to Denmark)

North
Sea

DENMARK

IRELAND

Isle
of Man
(to UK)

UNITED

KINGDOM

NETHERLANDS

BELGIUM

GERMANY

Channel
Islands
(to UK)

LUXEMBOURG

RE

ATLANTIC
OCEAN

FRANCE

LIECHTENSTEIN

AUST

SWITZERLAND

SL

SAN
MARINO

MONACO

I T A L

PORTUGAL

ANDORRA

VATICAN
CITY

S P A I N

Mediterranean
Sea

AFRICA

Asia

EUROPE

RUSSIA

TURKEY

GEORGIA

KAZAKHSTAN

CYPRUS

ARMENIA

AZERBAIJAN

UZBEKISTAN

LEBANON

AZERB.

SYRIA

ISRAEL

TURKMENISTAN

JORDAN

IRAQ

KYRGYZSTAN

TAJIKISTAN

IRAN

AFGHANISTAN

KUWAIT

SAUDI
ARABIA

BAHRAIN

PAKISTAN

QATAR

UNITED ARAB
EMIRATES

OMAN

YEMEN

INDIA

*Arabian
Sea*

AFRICA

*INDIAN
OCEAN*

↓ MALDIVES

SRI LANKA

Southeast Asia, Australia, and Oceania

ASIA

PACIFIC OCEAN

PACIFIC ISLANDS

MARSHALL ISLANDS
NAURU
TUVALU
KIRIBATI
SAMOA
TONGA

Guam (to USA)
Tokelau (to New Zealand)
Wallis & Futuna (to France)
American Samoa (to USA)
Niue (to New Zealand)
Cook Islands (to New Zealand)
French Polynesia (to France)
Pitcairn Islands (to UK)
Northern Mariana Islands (to USA)

MYANMAR (BURMA)
VIETNAM
LAOS
THAILAND
CAMBODIA

Philippine Sea

PHILIPPINES

South China Sea

MICRONESIA

PALAU

BRUNEI
MALAYSIA
SINGAPORE

INDONESIA

EAST TIMOR

Arafura Sea

PAPUA NEW GUINEA

SOLOMON ISLANDS

Timor Sea

Coral Sea

VANUATU

FIJI

INDIAN OCEAN

New Caledonia (to France)

AUSTRALIA

Great Australian Bight

Tasman Sea

NEW ZEALAND

North and South America

Canada

USA

Mexico

Guatemala

El Salvador

Honduras

Nicaragua

Costa Rica

Panama

Bahamas

Cuba

Jamaica

Puerto Rico
(to USA)

Belize

Colombia

Venezuela

Guyana

Suriname

Ecuador

Peru

Bolivia

Brazil

Paraguay

Uruguay

Chile

Argentina

Grenada

Haiti

St. Kitts &
Nevis

St. Lucia

St. Vincent &
Grenadines

Trinidad &
Tobago

Antigua &
Barbuda

Barbados

Dominica

Dominican
Republic

Europe

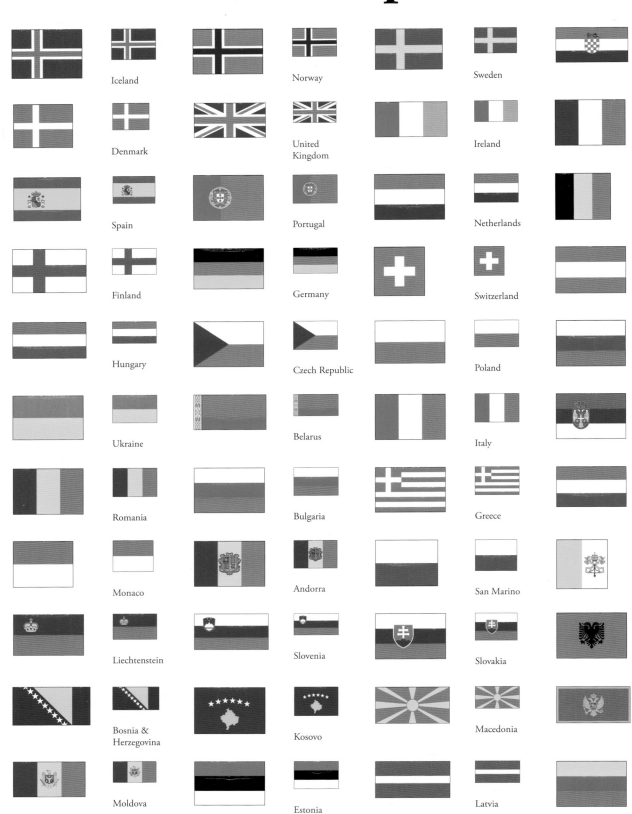

Iceland

Norway

Sweden

Croatia

Denmark

United Kingdom

Ireland

France

Spain

Portugal

Netherlands

Belgium

Finland

Germany

Switzerland

Austria

Hungary

Czech Republic

Poland

Russian Federation

Ukraine

Belarus

Italy

Serbia

Romania

Bulgaria

Greece

Luxembourg

Monaco

Andorra

San Marino

Vatican City

Liechtenstein

Slovenia

Slovakia

Albania

Bosnia & Herzegovina

Kosovo

Macedonia

Montenegro

Moldova

Estonia

Latvia

Lithuania

Cyprus

Malta

Africa

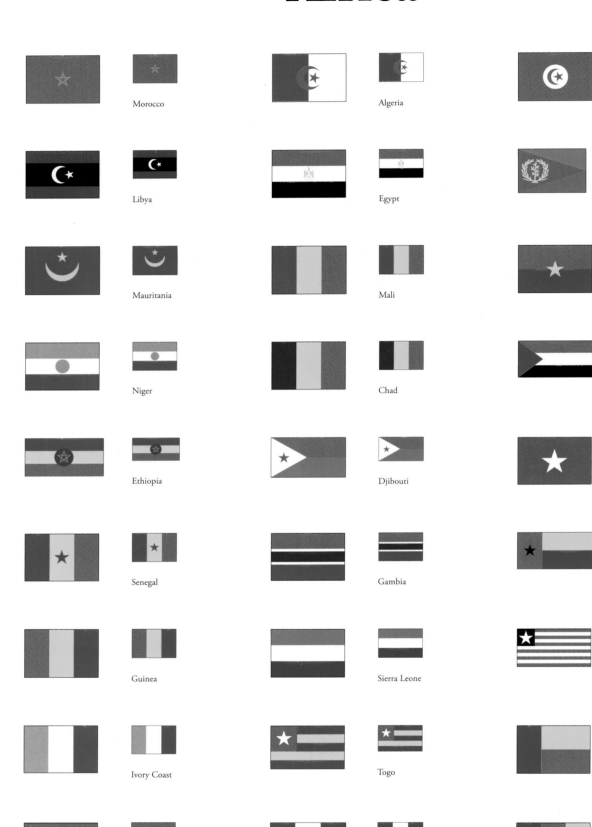

Morocco

Algeria

Tunisia

Libya

Egypt

Eritrea

Mauritania

Mali

Burkina Faso

Niger

Chad

Sudan

Ethiopia

Djibouti

Somalia

Senegal

Gambia

Guinea-Bissau

Guinea

Sierra Leone

Liberia

Ivory Coast

Togo

Benin

Ghana

Nigeria

Cameroon

Africa

Central African Republic

Equatorial Guinea

Gabon

Congo

Democratic Republic of the Congo

Uganda

Burundi

Kenya

Tanzania

Angola

Zambia

Malawi

Mozambique

Namibia

Botswana

Swaziland

Zimbabwe

Lesotho

South Africa

Madagascar

Rwanda

Cape Verde

Sao Tome & Principe

South Sudan

Mauritius

Seychelles

Comoros

Asia

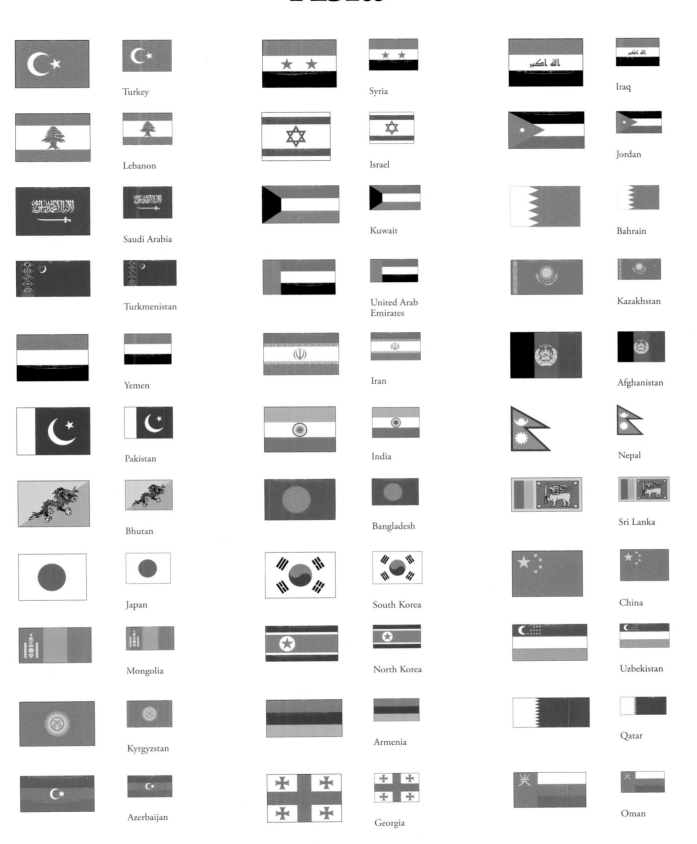

Turkey

Syria

Iraq

Lebanon

Israel

Jordan

Saudi Arabia

Kuwait

Bahrain

Turkmenistan

United Arab
Emirates

Kazakhstan

Yemen

Iran

Afghanistan

Pakistan

India

Nepal

Bhutan

Bangladesh

Sri Lanka

Japan

South Korea

China

Mongolia

North Korea

Uzbekistan

Kyrgyzstan

Armenia

Qatar

Azerbaijan

Georgia

Oman

Tajikistan

Maldives

Southeast Asia, Australia, and Oceania

Myanmar (Burma)

Thailand

Laos

Cambodia

Vietnam

Philippines

Malaysia

Singapore

Palau

Indonesia

Australia

Kiribati

Papua New Guinea

Tuvalu

Tonga

Marshall Islands

Solomon Islands

Micronesia

Fiji

Samoa

Nauru

New Zealand

Vanuatu

East Timor

Brunei

North America

ASIA

Beaufort
Sea

Alaska
(USA)

Greenland
(to Denmark)

Labrador
Sea

Hudson
Bay

CANADA

UNITED STATES
OF AMERICA

ATLANTIC
OCEAN

PACIFIC
OCEAN

MEXICO

Gulf of
Mexico

CARIBBEAN

Caribbean
Sea

BELIZE

GUATEMALA

HONDURAS

EL SALVADOR

NICARAGUA

SOUTH AMERICA

COSTA RICA

PANAMA

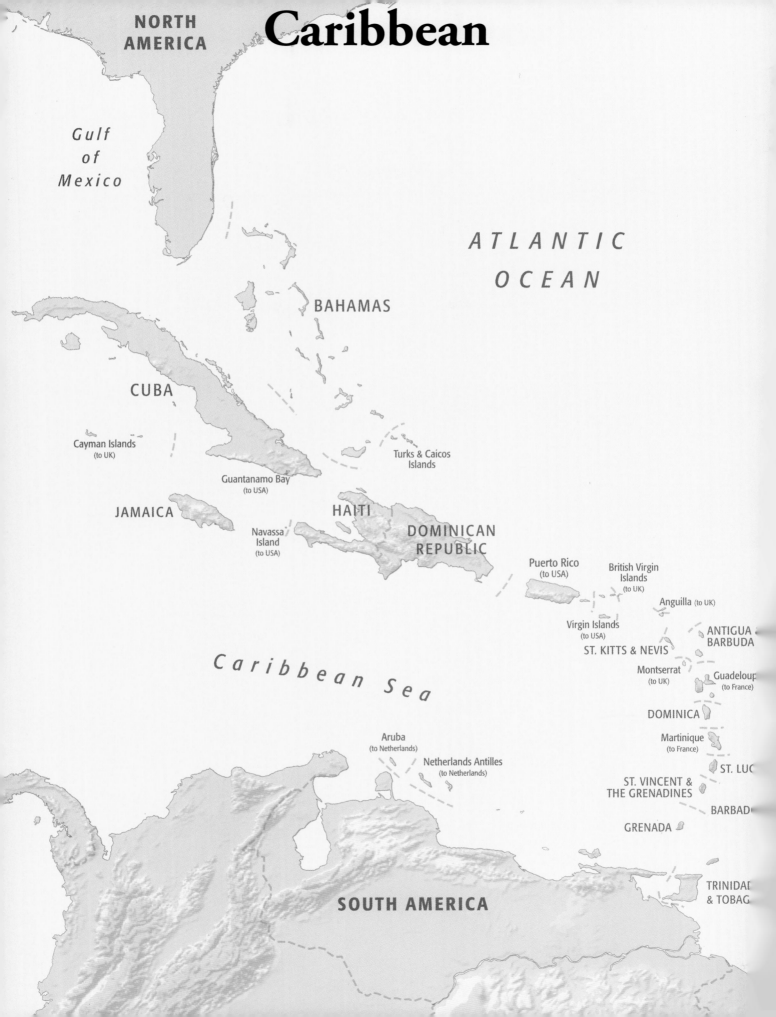

Caribbean

NORTH
AMERICA

*Gulf
of
Mexico*

ATLANTIC

OCEAN

BAHAMAS

CUBA

Cayman Islands
(to UK)

Turks & Caicos
Islands

Guantanamo Bay
(to USA)

JAMAICA

HAITI

DOMINICAN
REPUBLIC

Navassa
Island
(to USA)

Puerto Rico
(to USA)

British Virgin
Islands
(to UK)

Anguilla (to UK)

Virgin Islands
(to USA)

ANTIGUA
BARBUDA

ST. KITTS & NEVIS

Caribbean Sea

Montserrat
(to UK)

Guadeloup
(to France)

DOMINICA

Martinique
(to France)

Aruba
(to Netherlands)

Netherlands Antilles
(to Netherlands)

ST. LUC

ST. VINCENT &
THE GRENADINES

BARBAD

GRENADA

TRINIDAD
& TOBAG

SOUTH AMERICA

South America

NORTH
MERICA

VENEZUELA

GUYANA

SURINAME

French
Guiana
(to France)

COLOMBIA

ATLANTIC
OCEAN

ECUADOR

PERU

BRAZIL

BOLIVIA

PARAGUAY

PACIFIC

OCEAN

URUGUAY

CHILE   ARGENTINA

ATLANTIC

OCEAN

Falkland
Islands
(to UK)

Northern Africa

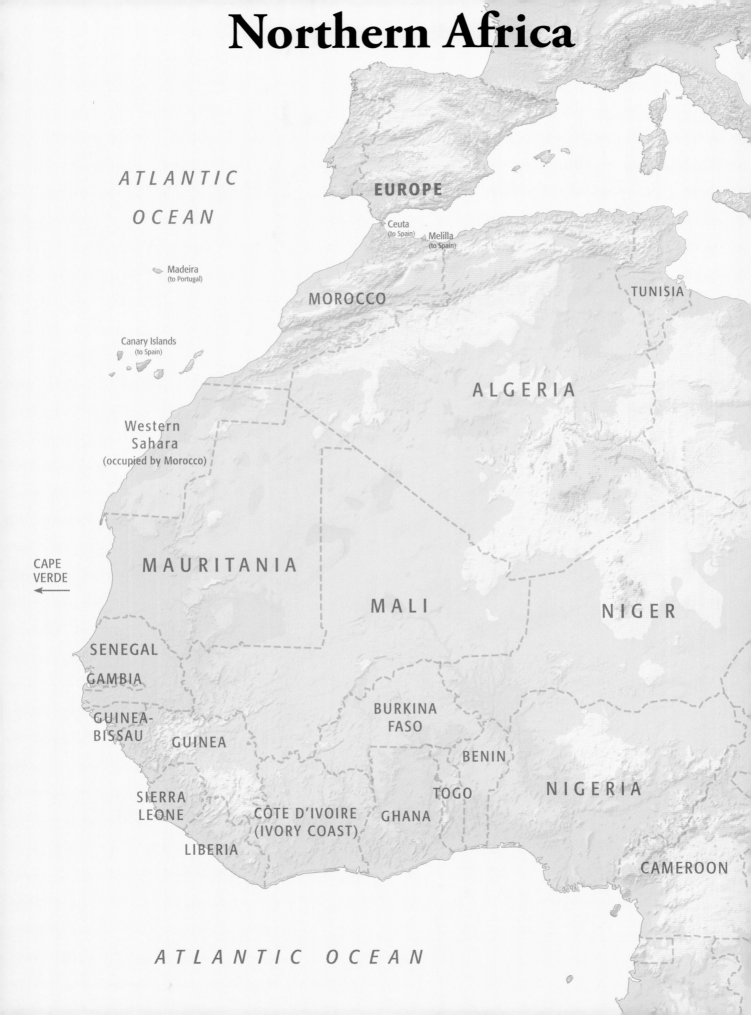

ATLANTIC

OCEAN

EUROPE

Ceuta
(to Spain)

Melilla
(to Spain)

Madeira
(to Portugal)

MOROCCO

TUNISIA

Canary Islands
(to Spain)

ALGERIA

Western
Sahara
(occupied by Morocco)

CAPE
VERDE

MAURITANIA

MALI

NIGER

SENEGAL

GAMBIA

GUINEA-
BISSAU

GUINEA

BURKINA
FASO

BENIN

NIGERIA

SIERRA
LEONE

CÔTE D'IVOIRE
(IVORY COAST)

TOGO

GHANA

LIBERIA

CAMEROON

ATLANTIC OCEAN

iterranean Sea

EGYPT

Red Sea

ASIA

SUDAN

ERITREA

Gulf of Aden

DJIBOUTI

SOMALIA

ETHIOPIA

SOUTH
SUDAN

AFRICAN
UBLIC

OUTHERN AFRICA

INDIAN

OCEAN

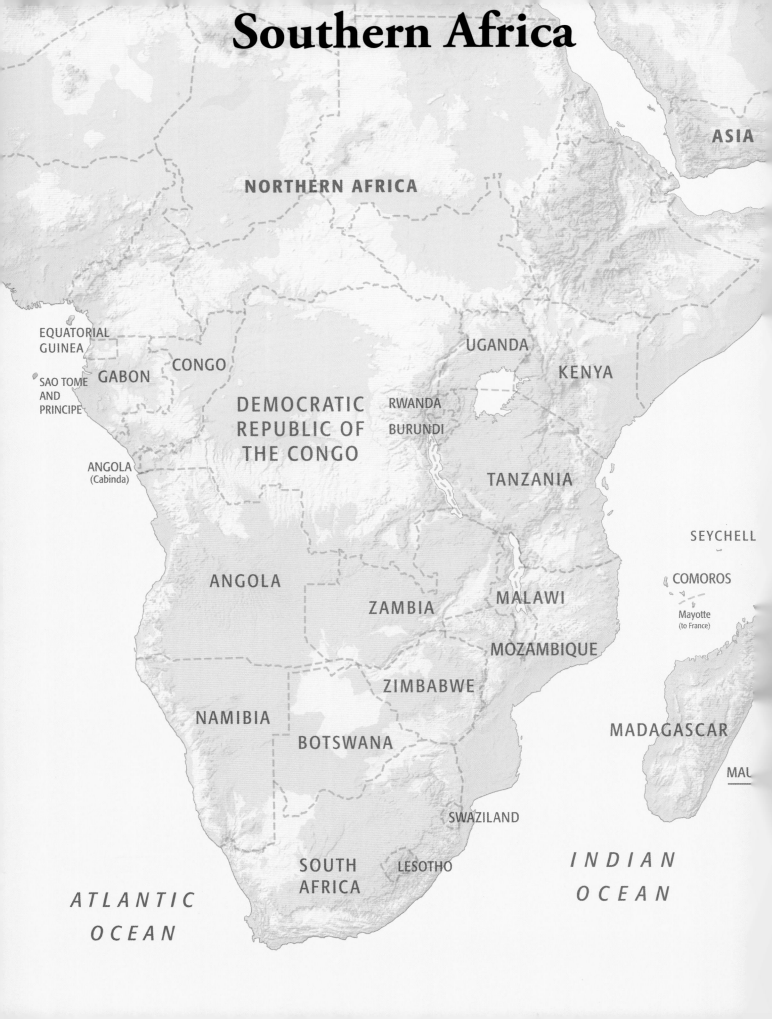

Southern Africa

ASIA

NORTHERN AFRICA

EQUATORIAL
GUINEA

SAO TOME
AND
PRINCIPE

GABON

CONGO

UGANDA

KENYA

DEMOCRATIC
REPUBLIC OF
THE CONGO

RWANDA

BURUNDI

ANGOLA
(Cabinda)

TANZANIA

SEYCHELL

COMOROS

ANGOLA

ZAMBIA

MALAWI

Mayotte
(to France)

MOZAMBIQUE

ZIMBABWE

NAMIBIA

MADAGASCAR

BOTSWANA

MAL

SWAZILAND

SOUTH
AFRICA

LESOTHO

INDIAN
OCEAN

ATLANTIC
OCEAN